Defining the Damages:
The Builder's Guide to Scope of Loss Reports

By Matthew Everson and Bill Wallace

Published by BW Builder
www.bwbuilder.com

Library of Congress Control Number: 9798985310603
ISBN: 979-8-9853106-0-3 (perfect bound paperback) |
979-8-9853106-1-0 (ebook)

Subjects: BISAC: TECHNOLOGY & ENGINEERING /
Construction/Estimating. | HOUSE & HOME / Design &
Construction. | HOUSE & HOME / Remodeling & Renovation

Opinions in this book must never be considered legal, tax, insurance, or
claims advice in any way. Always check our opinions with your
professional advisor. We share our knowledge only in the spirit of sharing
of information educationally.

Printed in the United States of America.

This book is written to honor the survivors of California wildfires. It is written to honor an initial promise made to United Policyholders (UP). Matt and Bill told Amy that one day, they would find a way to give away the 'secret sauce' of scope of loss reports. They felt it isn't right how some insurance companies put people through such anguish after a fire. They wanted to give UP another tool for their Roadmap to Recovery® program, as well as to give back to them for all they did to help Santa Rosa and the rest of California in the aftermath of our awful fires. To that end, proceeds from the sale of this book will benefit this charity with a 30+ year history of helping people understand their insurance rights.

With the purchase of this book, you are helping your town and this fine charity to continue their mission.

Thank you and good luck!

CONTENTS

Thank you for reading this book. By purchasing it, you are directly supporting United Policyholders, a charity that, for over 30 years, has helped people who are recovering from disasters. Proceeds from the sale of each book will go toward helping them continue their mission as independent advocates for those who have lost everything.

Forward

On a windy Sunday night back in October of 2017, thousands of residents of the small Northern California city of Santa Rosa became new members of an unfortunate club no one wants to be part of: disaster survivors. They'd soon learn that recovering from a large-scale wildfire is virtually impossible to do without help, and takes much longer than one might think.

This book was written by two of our volunteers, Bill Wallace and Matt Everson. In 2017, Matt and Bill were looking to help their city and neighbors emerge from economic and emotional wreckage after more than 5,000 homes were simultaneously destroyed. Neither one of them wanted to make a full-time career in the world of insurance and disaster recovery; they wanted to help the residents of Santa Rosa and move on with their lives and work. It was the Roadmap to Recovery® program that United Policyholders was putting on for the people of Santa Rosa that gave them an opportunity to lend some assistance.

United Policyholders is a non-profit that has been helping folks understand their insurance rights for over 30 years. While property insurance can and should be the fastest and best source of funds to repair and rebuild after a wildfire, those funds often don't flow as quickly or fully as they should. This is largely due to processes insurers have developed that they claim are designed to prevent fraud, but that can be maddening and deprive loss victims of funds they desperately need and are entitled to. Reaching an agreement on the replacement cost of a destroyed home is one of those challenging processes. This book offers a solution.

As builders, Bill and Matt knew that actual, local construction costs are a far more accurate indicator of repair and rebuild costs than the computer-generated estimates insurers typically use to make claim settlement offers. They also knew that home builders are in high demand after wildfires, and don't have the time to haggle with insurance adjusters over their estimates; this led them to develop a method for builders to prepare accurate and realistic rebuild estimates in a format that insurers should accept.

Because of their unique and forthright approach, their company, BW Builder, soon became a go-to when someone needed an accurate estimate of what the cost was to replace their destroyed home so they could reach a fair settlement with their insurance company.

Matt told me from the beginning he'd find a way to have their process somehow benefit United Policyholders' important charitable work. The result of that early promise is this book. In easy-to-understand language, BW Builder shares how other builders can adopt their system and help their communities rebuild after a wildfire. Their comprehensive methodology removes confusion, frustration, and questions from the process so wildfire-impacted homeowners can get their claims settled and focus on replacing what they've lost.

We appreciate that proceeds from the sale of this book will help United Policyholders further our mission of helping disaster survivors by serving as a trustworthy and useful information resource and a respected voice for consumers of all types of insurance in all 50 states. We look forward to continuing to help people and communities throughout the nation follow Matt and Bill's lead.

-Amy Bach, UP Executive Director

Prologue

The destruction and pain caused by wildfires is heartbreaking. It is bad enough to lose all your worldly possessions. But for many, a second disaster is right around the corner when it comes to dealing with trying to rebuild.

Why did we write a book about how builders can help? These wicked fires destroy homes and everything that was in them. Year after year, we see images on the TV of neighborhoods and forests decimated by fires and other natural disasters. Sadly, that list of destructive disasters continues to grow. But seeing these pictures on TV doesn't prepare people for the actual experience of seeing the damage from a disaster firsthand. It is a shock to the system.

The visceral impact of walking through a disaster zone is something someone can never forget. The desperate sight of neighborhoods erased and the chemical smell of still-smoldering piles of ash that once were homes leaves an unforgettable impact on one's psyche.

When the Tubbs fire burned over 5,000 homes in Santa Rosa back in October of 2017, Bill and Matt both experienced that shock. Being lucky to have their own homes spared, they began to ask how they could help in what seemed such a helpless situation. Have you asked yourself the same question? What can you do to help? To quote the Archbishop Desmond Tutu, "You show your humanity."

Amongst the cinders and ash, you will witness the kindness of neighbors helping friends dig through the debris. As the smoke clears, you will see charities like United Policyholders helping people understand their new life. And when it is time to rebuild, contractors will become heroes, rebuilding and getting people back in a new home.

This book is designed to help you help your neighbors by demystifying the most confusing aspects of the insurance claim process after a disaster. The authors shine a light on the unexpected yet important role builders and contractors can play in helping with an accurate rebuild estimate after a disaster like a wildfire. So many insurance claims get delayed due to homeowners being unable to give their insurance company accurate rebuild cost data in an acceptable format.

It isn't only individuals who are harmed by these disasters. The economic toll to the entire community is also extreme. One study found the damages from the 2018 California wildfires added up to over $148 billion in economic losses for the state. Some of those losses, such as tourism, property taxes, and people moving away are irreplaceable. But some losses are insured against, and this is where you can make a big impact on how quickly your town can get back on its feet.

The insurance claims process is confusing. That can lead to frustration, which can lead many people to give up and leave paid-for insurance benefits on the table. That is money your community will never see again. It is also money that won't go into rebuilds. You can help people get this money!

After a home is lost to fire, it is the loss survivor's (claimant's) duty to report the financial price of the loss to their insurance company. That financial price is called the "measure of indemnity" and it unlocks everything in a claim. Basically: How much will it cost to rebuild the home that was lost? While no one is better suited to determine that value than a builder familiar with local building standards and costs, putting those figures in a format that an insurance company will accept can be a frustrating endeavor.

Early on, Bill and Matt decided they wouldn't go from town to town, year after year, reliving devastation in other communities. They decided that after Santa Rosa claims were settled, they would come up with a way to put this business "in a bottle" (they are from wine country, after all) to allow other character-driven builders and citizens to help their own cities recover from a disaster using the same process that BW Builder used to help get Santa Rosa back on its feet.

The objective of this book is to benefit your community and United Policyholders by sharing how Bill and Matt found a way to unlock this mess. If builders can help disaster survivors rebuild faster, the entire community will recover faster, both economically and emotionally.

Chapter 1 – Helping Your Town Rebuild*

Chapter Summary:

✓ The formats used by builders to estimate costs are not formats accepted by insurance companies.

✓ The insurance companies have intentionally left their claims process ambiguous. Use that against them. Unless they give you written guidelines, they have no grounds to reject an accurate rebuild estimate from a local, licensed builder.

✓ Don't ask "why" an insurance company does what it does. It is a time-wasting endeavor, and you need to get going! Follow the steps in this book.

✓ Insurance companies require details on the cost and quantity of the materials, labor, and code upgrades required for the build; far more details than you are used to providing.

✓ A builder is the only expert that can provide the accuracy and details required for a rebuild estimate after a wildfire. If you learn to give those details in an acceptable format, your neighbors can get the money they need to pay you to start building.

How do contractors usually come up with rebuild estimates and bids to build a home? Many use the tried-and-true method of quoting a price per square foot. Some use a 16d format or other similar software. **The important thing to take from this chapter is that the estimating methods you have used your entire career do not provide enough detail for an insured to settle a claim.** Whichever method you use for your estimates, you don't spend 10-20 hours compiling a 50-page price breakdown describing every nail, labor hour, and piece of wood that will go into the build. Why would you?

The fact that you don't have the time to put such an estimate together might be why insurance companies demand such detail - if a builder can't provide it, no one else can. If no one else can provide an alternative to the estimates insurance companies are providing, disaster survivors have a big problem: they can't properly reflect their loss, and that leads to lower claims payouts.

Without an accurate estimate created by someone knowledgeable about building in your area, a wildfire survivor can't prove the real rebuild costs of the home they lost and may not receive all the money they deserve from their insurance coverage.

That's where you come in: if you can help your clients give their insurance company better pricing data on rebuilds after a disaster, you will be a hero for your clients and your town. In preparing just under 100 such estimates for people in Santa Rosa after the 2017 fires, we were able to unlock an estimated

$60 million of insurance proceeds that companies had initially denied paying out. As of the publishing date of this book, we have prepared over 200 estimates and unlocked over $110 million of previously denied insurance proceeds for people in cities across California that have been devastated by wildfires.

A note of warning: Insurance fraud goes as far back to the days when insurance first became a business in the 1700s. From the very first days, people have been claiming they lost more than they actually did. Thus, to protect themselves against paying out too much, the insurance companies seek proof of the losses. They produce estimates for their customers, but those estimates are done by in-house adjusters or construction companies with little knowledge of the building codes and pricing in the area where the disaster occurred. In our experience, more often than not, those estimates are materially deficient in both pricing and scope of the build.

For many claimants, those insurance company-provided estimates spark anxiety. The concern is caused when disaster survivors begin speaking with local builders and realize the estimate they got from their insurance adjuster is 20-50% lower than the actual costs they will incur. How will they be able to rebuild? How can anyone enter a contract to build if the estimated rebuild cost from their insurance company (essentially, what the company believes the claimant is owed) is 30%-50% below local builder bids? Your neighbors need the ability to counter an inaccurate insurance company estimate with a more accurate estimate of their own from a local builder.

This guide is a step-by-step explanation of how to create that estimate to help claimants provide the data needed to finalize their claims.

The economic windfall coming your way as a builder in a community recently wrecked by disaster may turn out to be the most profitable building period of your career. **Give back to that fortunate happenstance.**

In the end, if you can help reduce the frustration, delays, and mental anguish that so many survivors go through, it will mean that money enters the local economy quicker, people are re-housed sooner, and the emotional and financial toll that these disasters enact can be lessened.

Can you take some time to give back to your community?

* Opinions in this book must never be considered legal, tax, insurance, or claims advice in any way. Always check our opinions with your professional advisor. We share our knowledge only in the spirit of sharing of information educationally.

Chapter 2 - The Basics of a Claim*

Chapter Summary:

✓ "Claims make no sense!" We know. They probably never will. Don't ask why!

✓ The cost for all aspects of the rebuild is called "Measure of Indemnity" or MOI.

✓ Create a quality estimate (also called a Scope of Loss Report) focused on the cost to rebuild the home that was lost, not the replacement home to be built.

✓ Perform an honest, accurate estimate, and your client has a tool the insurance companies have a hard time refuting.

✓ Use the "Tips from Bill and Matt" at the end of the chapter to help folks get the claim done!

This Claims Process Makes No Sense!

Insurance adjusters have a process. However, they typically won't share that process with you (or anyone). While every company's process will differ, they seem to share one common theme: their policy is vague about how to demonstrate your Measure of Indemnity (MOI). **This chapter shows how you can help your clients better establish their MOI.** Because companies refuse to be specific about the claims process, we feel it is reasonable to use their generalities against them. **If they won't tell you precisely what they need from you, how can they possibly tell you the estimate that you've provided isn't acceptable?**

The Basics of a Claim

Here is what you need to know: **The insurance company insured the home that was lost or damaged, not the one you will build to replace it.** To build a proper scope of loss report, you must start with understanding how the home was built before the fire, flood, or hurricane. *For now, forget about the new home or repairs that will be built tomorrow.* Focus on how much it would cost to replace what was lost the day of the disaster. You are going to estimate what that damaged or lost home, built to current codes, would cost to rebuild.

The insurance company needs to verify what was lost and how much it will cost to be replaced. That means labor and materials, along with soft costs like architectural and engineering. Don't forget to include your profits. Remember the MOI, or loss value? This is one of the most important parts of the client's claim: **what will it cost to replace what was lost?** Your estimate will help your clients establish their MOI with their insurance company.

Companies like BW Builder do the scope of loss report for a fee. If you're like us, you'll charge a price close to the type of price an engineer charges for one of their reports: $2,000 to $10,000 seems fair. The idea here is not to fleece the disaster survivor. We feel like smart builders will bake this cost into their overhead. However, if you're doing it for someone for whom you are not building, it is fair to be compensated for your time. Draw up a contract, quote a cost, build the estimate.

Insurance rules differ by state. No matter your state, insurance companies all need basic data like local labor rates, material costs (chapter 3), code upgrades (chapter 4), and your profits and overhead, all detailed in an estimate. If you build an accurate estimate (also called a Scope of Loss Report) that clearly depicts the loss and the cost to replace that loss, it will be difficult for the companies to argue that their estimate is better than yours. At this point your client can demand their insurance company agree on their MOI (the total rebuild cost) and become comfortable entering a contract to build. They will need to push hard to obtain that MOI agreement in writing.

Note: An estimated MOI will never equal the final MOI. You will only ever have the final MOI when the build is complete. You are simply seeking to have the company realize their estimate is deficient (on labor, materials, and code changes), and yours better represents what was there and what it will cost to rebuild. The local builder is the expert, not the out-of-town adjuster.

Claimants will often have to go back and forth with the insurance company over the estimate because they often do not like figures that are higher than their own. That haggling will be frustrating and may take the patience of a saint, but eventually you and your client can compel the company to accept your cost estimate over theirs. **You are the subject matter expert in construction for your community and you have data to back up your estimated costs.** They are neither experts at building in your area, nor do they have good data. With better data and a more accurate estimate, you and your clients win.

Once there is agreement on MOI, everything else can fall into place.

Not getting an agreement on MOI is where many survivors get stuck. They feel that they can't sign a six- or seven-figure fixed-bid contract with a builder if they aren't sure how much their company will cover. Can you blame them? Once clients know how much coverage is available, they can get off the bump. With an MOI agreed upon, they can sign a contract with you and get started on the replacement house.

Note: Your insurance company adjuster will probably never mention the term MOI. They may even pretend not to know what you're talking about. It doesn't matter. Tell them that you know that they know what MOI means. Be specific in writing to them about it. You need them to agree that your estimate is accurate and represents the best estimate of MOI.

One of many maddening things about this process is that every claim is different. That said, much of it is universal. The bottom line is that the company needs proof, in a format they will accept, that the six- or seven-figure check they are going to write your client is based on realistic data.

Tips from Matt and Bill:

1. <u>Be realistic and business-like</u>. The insurance company does not care about the disaster as much as you and your client. It isn't personal. They have too many cases. They don't live there. They have no idea what people are going through. While some adjusters may be empathetic, they are forced to weigh being nice, helpful, or friendly with what their employer demands.

The claim adjuster is a human stuck in a difficult job. If you really want to slow down the case, return their lack of friendliness. Otherwise, do your best to remain professional. **Do not yell, don't name-call, don't swear.** We tried; we can assure you it doesn't work! When they tell you the numbers don't look right, they aren't accusing you of lying. They are attempting to understand how your numbers are so much higher than the one their software gives them. The claim adjuster did not make the ridiculous rules of this game, they are just trying to do their job and get through their workday. Stick to the facts, stay calm, and be as nice as you can.

2. <u>Be laser-focused on getting the company to agree upon the MOI</u>. Your client needs to ask for that exact thing, in writing. The companies may hem and haw but if your client repeatedly asks for an agreement on loss value and the company refuses to discuss it, your client may have evidence of bad faith dealing. One of the few areas an insurance company can be held liable for violating the law is "bad faith." Use it sparingly, but document all instances where an adjuster misleads or misrepresents a situation.

3. <u>Ask the right questions</u>. Any time you ask a question, if you don't get a clear answer, ask it a different way. Try different verbs and words. Do this on email and on the phone. If they refer you to the policy, politely ask them, "Precisely which page and paragraph are you referring to in the policy?" Keep asking questions. Adjusters often shade things or tell vague truths. Be nice but firm. **If it isn't in writing and in the policy or the insurance code of your state, then it isn't important. If they cannot produce written proof of the position they have staked out, politely tell them to stop misdirecting things and begin adherence to the policy and laws.**

4. <u>Be Organized</u>. Stay focused on one to two things per call or email. Always write down notes on a phone call including date, time, and who you spoke with. Write down the phone numbers, the people on the call, and what the call was about. Any time money is mentioned or a promise made verbally, email a recap of the call or discussion back to your client and the adjuster. In this world, if it isn't in writing, it didn't happen. Adjusters often prefer to discuss everything about the claim over the phone. If that is the case, always send a detailed email recap of the call to the adjuster and to the claimant. That makes it more difficult for an adjuster to back out of any verbal commitments that were made on the call.

5. Put a Date on It. Be brief and specific when asking for something. Put a date on each request. For example: "Dear Adjuster, Thanks for your time today. On the call, we discussed that ABC Insurance wants details on plumbing subcontractor building costs. If the details attached to this email aren't sufficient, we request your reply, in writing, as to what specifically is needed, no later than next **Wednesday, June 21, 2021**." Placing a date on the request or question (with a reasonable timeframe for the request) is a little secret you'll want to employ.

The "date by" request means the adjuster will calendar that request versus waiting until you call or email again to get on it. It means that should they not reply by that date, your client may have some evidence for proving bad faith dealing.

The adjuster knows this, too. They have been trained to reply by deadlines. Often, the reply will be "I haven't had time to get you the answer you want." But they can only use that excuse so many times before evidence of bad faith begins to pile up.

If they cannot comply with your request by the given date, be stern and ask them to give you the exact time they will comply with the request.

6. Be Honest. This may be your first time dealing with insurance companies in this fashion, but they deal with crooks all the time. If you think there's a scheme you can pull off, they've already seen it. Once they peg you as someone trying to fudge numbers, this process becomes nearly impossible.

Always remember that all of this may one day be called into a court of law, and you will be asked to prove all your figures. If you can't prove the costs you are using in your estimate (your own invoices from builds, subcontractor bids from the past, phone calls to other builders and supply stores, price lists from supply stores), don't bother making an estimate. These companies can smell a ruse from a mile away. Do the estimate the right way. Be honest.

7. <u>Get them what they need</u>! The company needs proof of the loss. They need a detailed cost breakdown. They will typically provide one of their own estimates, which will often reflect a lower cost-to-build: we have seen estimates from insurance companies that show a rebuild cost that is 40% below the actual cost to rebuild. You can either help your client correct that estimate (if you understand Xactimate estimates) or formulate a more accurate one in either Xactimate or any other format that gives them adequate detail. BW Builder has an easy-to-use Excel spreadsheet that is available at their www.bwbuilder.com website.

The company may simply accept your estimate. But they may also ask you to provide them with invoices for materials, labor, or subcontractor costs, from past jobs. Show them proof supporting the numbers in the estimate. If they ask and you have no data to support your costs, your estimate can't be counted as accurate.

Another important point: your client knows you aren't building the home for free, so be sure and show where you've factored a profit and overhead into your figures in the estimate. It's sometimes more than 20% of the overall cost and needs to be included as part of the MOI.

Opinions in this book must never be considered legal, tax, insurance, or claims advice in any way. Always check our opinions with your professional advisor. We share our knowledge only in the spirit of sharing of information educationally.

Chapter 3 – How to Create an Acceptable Estimate*

Chapter Summary:

✓ Get as much detail on the old home as possible – blueprints, plans, photos, and descriptions from the client and city or county.

✓ Insurance policies do not usually describe what is required from a scope of loss report. Use that ambiguity to your advantage.

✓ There is no law, insurance code, or policy provision we are aware of that requires a specific format or software for a scope of loss report. Do not let an adjuster try to tell you otherwise.

✓ Have your client review a draft and find out where the estimate needs to be adjusted to better reflect the home that was lost.

✓ Send it to the insurance adjuster with a cover letter requesting that the company agree upon your estimated rebuild cost as the claimant's measure of indemnity.

We know of two ways to go about creating an acceptable estimate:

1) Pay for a license with the company that owns Xactimate, learn their cumbersome system, then learn how to create your own pricing in their system when and if you discover their numbers for labor and materials don't match the reality of your area.

2) Download the spreadsheet we have designed with a real builder in mind. If you know how to use Microsoft Excel (or someone in your office does), there is only a small learning curve. Go to www.bwbuilder.com for more information.

In either case, you are performing the same function: using software to produce an estimate. You just need to choose how you want to format your estimate.

The first step is to get any and all details you can on the home that was damaged or lost. You don't need the original building plans, but they definitely help! If those aren't available, help the client sketch the floor plan. You need a description of the home, room by room. You need to know the layout of the home in order to fill in the data.

The second step, if it is safe (burn sites have a lot of risk to injury – be prepared with safety shoes, proper gear, a mask, and gloves) and you won't be violating any post-disaster access restrictions for access, go measure the house yourself. A lot of folks think they can just base their estimate off the measurements an insurance company adjuster took. If you do that, don't be surprised if your estimate is rejected. Establish your own scope of loss. Ask the client to give you photos, videos, written descriptions, and/or anything else that can describe their home.

Note: we have heard adjusters tell claimants to use an architect to draw up plans – for the destroyed home. In our opinion, this is a frustration tactic. There is no need to spend money on renderings from an architect for a home that will not be built. This is an estimate you're creating. The claimant should save their money for an architect's drawings of the home that will eventually be rebuilt.

The third step is to put that intake data to work! Whichever software you choose to use, this is where your building expertise comes in. Room by room, you will need to recreate that old home. Line by line, you will need to list the materials and labor needed for each room. This includes boards, joists, nails, labor hours, and *everything* else.

Xactimate will calculate that labor for you. **But be careful!** The data contained in the software is not always perfect. Labor hours needed on a job often do not match what you know will be needed as an expert builder. Also, the pricing of that labor will vary in accuracy, sometimes wildly. BW Estimator has you enter the local dollar amounts for materials and labor.

You can use your own payroll, sub-contractor invoices, and phone calls to local peers to establish your labor pricing. You can use invoices you've recently paid as the basis for material costs. Many contractor supply stores now have price lists available online. Download those and compare them to your own figures. Call the stores if pricing isn't available online. Essentially, you need to create a small research file that demonstrates you aren't pulling figures out of thin air.

Now the not so fun part: data entry. In either software, you must type in the data. It takes a fair amount of time, which is why no one should do this for free. Enter the data, line by line, room by room. You can go to our website to see a few examples of what an estimate looks like when complete in Xactimate and what it looks like in BW Estimator.

You will need to estimate the home from top to bottom. This isn't a bid for business. Imagine you are explaining, section by section, how a home gets built. You're explaining it on paper, room by room. You will also include rough plumbing and electrical, framing, foundation, basement, walls, roof, flooring, trim, and anything else that would stay attached to the home if you could pick it up and shake it; all of it needs a line item. Imagine that your estimate needs be approved by your local building permit department. Would it pass? Once you have accomplished this, go sit with the client for an hour and go over the draft. Review the things they can remember like flooring, doors, windows, tile, etc. They will likely find a few items that need to be adjusted, i.e. too many/too few windows.

Once you've made the necessary corrections, it's done. It can be helpful to add some documents that pertain to local building codes, any news articles describing price fluctuations in the area, and/or any findings from local or state emergency agencies that might help an adjuster understand local building and insurance codes. We will often include photos and a bit of information about us and why our estimate can be viewed as honest and accurate. You can do this, too.

At this point, it is the client's job to send the estimate to their insurance company (email is fine) with a cover letter that specifically asks for an agreement on the measure of indemnity (MOI) **and a specific 'reply by' date** from their adjuster so the company doesn't drag their feet in the review.

Insurance companies often will not provide clear claims guidelines. Use this against them. If they balk at any estimate, you or your client must ask them what the rejection is based on. Is it somewhere in the policy? Where, exactly? Have the claimant demand that they put any objections to the estimate in a detailed, written response.

In response, an insurance company may ask you to defend your pricing or construction expertise. Don't take it personally; simply supply them with the data you have. This should all be done in writing. Do not take their objections over the phone. Ask that they put their questions and concerns in writing and in detail. Specifically, which page of the estimate, which section, and which line item is in question and what is their question.

Also, along with their response in writing, demand that they give you and your client the source of their material and labor data. Typically, their data comes from Xactimate, and can often be wildly different from local pricing data after a disaster. In contrast, you can prove what the sub-contractor just charged you. Can they find someone to frame a home at the rate the software claims? Ask them.

For example, in early 2022, the Xactimate software labor rate for framing in Sonoma County, CA was showing $4 per square foot. Calling around to any builder to verify this, you'd hear lots of laughter. The going rate for framing in February 2022 was anywhere from $25 to $50 per hour. You can begin to see why insurance company estimates often fail to accurately portray the real costs to rebuild.

If you create a good report and the company rejects it (initially they will usually claim it isn't sufficient or your pricing is too high), many state insurance codes have a provision that says something to the effect that if an insurance company rejects a loss estimate, they must provide a detailed and written response as to why they rejected it. Be sure not to get into this dispute on the phone. If they won't initially accept your estimate, ask them to state, **in writing**, exactly which line items they disagree with and why. Take and read that written description and correct your estimate or their mistakes. Avoid arguing, yelling, or verbal confrontation. Ask for their reasons in writing, and craft your response in writing. If they won't respond to repeated requests in writing, it only gives a claimant more content for their "dealing in bad faith" evidence folder.

Don't participate in padding estimates or invoices. Insurance companies take fraud very seriously. Clients may push you to inflate the costs, but they do not deserve a penny over their measure of indemnity. Insurance is a business, and claims are not free money. Your best option is to be honest in your estimates. The penalties for fraud are serious, and include jail time, fines, and loss of licensure. Your job is to build a home and make a profit. There are enough liars in this marketplace; by being honest and helping the customer with the tool they need to settle their claim, you will help clients resolve claims more rapidly and be able to get to rebuilding their home.

The ball is now in your client's court: they need to push the insurance company for an agreement on the MOI. With your solid estimate, they can get to the MOI and you can all get to rebuilding their replacement home!

*Opinions in this book must never be considered legal, tax, insurance, or claims advice in any way. Always check our opinions with your professional advisor. We share our knowledge only in the spirit of sharing of information educationally.

Chapter 4 - Code Upgrades*

Chapter Summary:

✓ Every three years, the Universal Building Code (UBC) is updated with new rules for building. Most states follow the UBC and implement the updates every three years.

✓ This means the older the home that was lost in the disaster, the more changes will be required to rebuild it. The costs related to upgrading it from where it was to meet current code are called Code Upgrades.

✓ This is a very subjective and ambiguous area of insurance.

✓ Xactimate does not attempt to include Code Upgrades in their software.

✓ You will want to work with local architects and the county or city building department to develop a basic list of the upgrades from the last 20 years.

✓ You then need to estimate what it would have cost to install the old item (e.g., 50-gallon water heater would have been $1,200), what the upgrade cost is (e.g., on-demand heater will be $2,400), and then calculate the difference. In this example, the Code Upgrade cost is $1,200.

Code Upgrades are difficult to estimate (yet another area we suspect is designed ambiguity). Code Upgrade coverage (sometimes called Ordinance & Law) is sold as a benefit. Yet when the time comes to claim the damages, companies will often give no guidance on how to obtain this coverage. As we wrote in the "Tips" section of the previous chapter, ask the company to be specific about what they need. Usually, they won't have anything for you to refer to, but you still want to have your questions and their answers in writing for your file.

What are Code Upgrades? In essence, a Code Upgrade, for the purposes of this discussion, is the added cost to the rebuild or repair of a damaged home due to the changes in building codes since the time the house was built.

For example, homes built in the 1990s had 40- or 50-gallon gas water heaters. Today, due to energy efficiency codes in California, a newly installed water heater is likely to be a more expensive "on-demand" system. Whereas the 50-gallon water heater might be $1,200 to buy and install, the on-demand system is $2,400. In this example, if the client has Code Upgrade coverage, she could potentially claim a $1,200 Code Upgrade expense.

In your estimate, you will want to provide a table for the insurance adjuster. Each state (and now even city and county) may have its unique additions to the UBC. It can be helpful to reach out to an architect or the county building commission and ask them to look at your list to see if you're missing something.

Your table should look something like this:

Item	Original Construction	Actual Cost Due to Code Upgrades	Code Upgrade Added Cost	Code Requirement
Water Heater	$1200	$2400	$1200	Req'd by Title 24 part 6 (CEC)

Think of this table as an addendum. Xactimate does not have a feature to break out Code Upgrade expenses. BW Builder hired a few retired adjusters from large insurance companies to get insider information on what the companies need to see. We learned we need to break out the "Code Upgrade costs" as a portion of the overall cost. **Code Upgrade costs are not additional costs.** Of a $1,000,000 rebuild, if $100,000 is attributed to Code Upgrades, that doesn't mean the cost to build is $1.1 million. It means the rebuild will cost $1 million and of that $1 million, $100k is attributed to Code Upgrades.

Having a coverage category for Code Upgrades but no guidance on how to determine costs associated with it is highly frustrating for claimants. Without a good way to prove the added costs of Code Upgrades, people will often give up and leave money that they deserve on the table.

Gather with the local builder's exchange, civil engineers, architects, and the city and county to come up with a list of changes that have occurred over the years for your area. Check

United Policyholders, websites for cities of past fires like Santa Rosa, Paradise, and others to pull a list together.

Share that list with all builders and disaster survivors who need it. Email us for our list, but it is only a starting point, as it is only for California (but may be applicable to your state). You'll want to work on it further with the groups named above to be certain you've got the best data.

Some other thoughts:

1) Code Upgrades typically only apply when you choose to rebuild or replace, but the rules vary by policy and state. In other words, if the client isn't rebuilding the home or replacing it by purchasing another one, they will usually not qualify for Code Upgrade coverage.

Reach out to your state's department of insurance for the Code Upgrade rules pertaining to insurance. The insurance company adjuster will typically not be from your state and will not have the answer to "What qualifies as a Code Upgrade?" They will usually default to "The claim doesn't qualify for that money." You are a builder, you know the code; work with the city or county and determine the code changes that have been instituted over the last few decades.

2) Don't be tempted by greed. As it is an ambiguous area, many folks think this is free money if they can just scheme up a spreadsheet. As unlikely as it may be, you might have to defend this document in court or arbitration one day. In over 200

cases, only one of our estimates has gone to arbitration (which we won). That's because our figures are accurate and we can back them up. If you can't substantiate your reasons for the estimate, you lose. You cannot make this stuff up, and you cannot fool an insurance company; just do your estimates right and it all works so much better.

3) In California and many other states, insurance adjusters will tell claimants they only get this coverage if they rebuild. But when you read Section 2105.5 of the California insurance code, you can see this doesn't seem to be true in California. The Code Upgrade figure is part of your overall measure of indemnity. **DO NOT TAKE AN ADJUSTER'S WORD ON THIS TOPIC!** Go research it on a website like www.uphelp.org.

If you purchase our BW Estimator software, you have the beginnings of the list you'll need. Work with local architects, engineers, and county planners to flesh out more details for your area.

* Opinions in this book must never be considered legal, tax, insurance, or claims advice in any way. Always check our opinions with your professional advisor. We share our knowledge only in the spirit of sharing of information educationally.

Chapter 5 - Frequently Asked Questions*

1. Why would any builder want to spend time on an estimate when there are so many homes to build?

Most builders will not want to do this. The majority will be too busy building and not be inclined to want to do anything else after a disaster.

But we have faith there will be at least a few builders, and hopefully the local builder's exchange, a local Rotary Club, or an entrepreneur in each town affected by wildfires or other disasters that will want to serve their community.

Disasters are not only damaging to the folks who lose property; they wreck the entire community, both emotionally and economically.

If you can help survivors get the funds that they deserve from insurance more quickly, you will be helping to ease their individual anxiety while helping the economy of your community to rebound.

2. What is the best way to prove the measure of indemnity (value of loss)?

First ask your client to ask their adjuster what exactly they want to see in an estimate. Ask the adjuster to be as specific as possible and place those requirements in writing. It isn't likely to result in much, as they are not known to be helpful guides in this area but if they don't provide many details, their ambiguity here can be helpful.

If they refuse to provide any details, how can they reject any format you provide them? On what basis? Ask them to provide their answer in writing.

Tip: Ask questions in different ways. Try asking different questions if the adjuster is being too general:

- Do you have a detailed claims procedure you can send to me via email?
- What documents will you accept to prove the value of loss?
- Will you please email a list of documents you will accept to prove the value of loss?
- Can you be more specific in what you need?
- Do you have any examples of an acceptable estimate you can share?

These are all questions that can be asked by the claimant or yourself if you are their builder. If you aren't in contract to build their home, they will typically only speak with the claimant, so if this is your situation, share these tips with the insured.

If the adjuster won't be specific, we believe that allows a claimant to provide data on their own terms. If the company later balks, ask them on what basis they cannot accept something if they have no process to share in the first place?

3. Can I create my own Xactimate report?

Anyone can purchase a license to the software and pay the company's subscription fee. Builders can do this if they have time to learn the software.

Even with extensive experience, accurate reports take 10-20 hours to create in the software. If you have never used Xactimate, it might be a better idea to find help. We encourage builders to try BW Estimator. Our spreadsheet was designed with a builder in mind. Anyone in your office that knows the basics of Excel spreadsheets can use BW Estimator.

As the previous question just pointed out, the insurance companies refuse to give guidelines. There is nowhere, in any policy that we are aware of, that states the estimate must be done in any format whatsoever. If you're only going to do a few of these to help your community or friends, why go to the expense and time it takes to use Xactimate properly when the office manager you have already knows how to use Excel?

4. What are best practices for a contractor in a claims process?

See our tips at the end of Chapter 2. Here are more:

- Do your best to capture all conversations in writing.
- Date each conversation and note who you were speaking with and what was said.
- Handling everything in writing is best practice.
- Be sure to send a copy of any correspondence or conversation with an insurance adjuster to your client.
- Title each email with a new subject line for each topic to keep things straight. Don't reply to a months-long string of emails. You won't be able to find the things you want as easily.
- Always state the exact date you need their reply. Give them a reasonable amount of time to reply but **always** have a "reply by" date. Always put "Please reply no later than _____," and put a specific time and day in the blank.
- Do not count on the insurance company to honor anything said over the phone or in conversation with you. They may state "the call is being recorded" but if the call goes against them, the company may not be able to find the recording.
- If you do have a conversation with an adjuster over the phone, best practice is to write them an email reiterating everything said in the phone conversation and CC your client right after you hang up. In the email, ask the adjuster to confirm that the conversation took place. Don't forget your "reply by" date.

- Create a research and price file in your office. Keep track of your sub-contractor invoices and keep track of your own. When requested, provide those to insurance companies with pictures of completed work, city or county sign-offs, and any other aspects of the build. That way, if the company asks (and they might), you can easily get them the proof they need to support the estimate you have created.
- Be patient.
- Be helpful.
- Don't add to the stress.

5. Can a contractor help claimants with insurance claims?

Yes! And it is in both the client's and your best interest to work together to settle the claim. As we have described, a builder can provide the missing link – proof of loss in a scope of loss report – to help move the claim along. Do not do this work for free. It can be time-consuming, and it is fair to charge a reasonable price for your time. A preliminary agreement of payment should be made beforehand. Ask your client to understand that you will only be able to do so much since you are used to building houses, not dealing with insurance companies. **Don't give advice on insurance**. Focus on estimating the rebuild costs. Being able to get the client a dependable, accurate scope of loss report is 99% more than most builders will do.

6. What kind of data do I ask a client for to create a good scope of loss report?

Chapter 3 discusses this in-depth. In short, details. The more details they can provide for the house that was damaged, the better.

Best practice is to go room by room and collect the details of the finish, windows, doors, flooring, and other items like fireplaces, etc.

Gather any pictures and/or invoices of any upgrades they made to the home over the years and try to secure the original building plans. If there are no plans, take notes on the home from the client, including any specialty items on the house. Sketch out a simple floor plan of the home with dimensions if actual plans aren't available.

Remember, you are estimating the home that was damaged or lost as if you were rebuilding it (to current code) today. **You aren't focused on the one they will build to replace the lost home.** Any details you can dig up on the home will help create the most accurate valuation of loss and will help the client make their case.

You'll have to document the cost of all aspects of the home, from the bones and the skin to foundation to roof and every wall in between. Each of the software programs we have mentioned guide you room by room.

7. When I have completed the first draft of the estimate, what should I do?

Give a copy to your client and ask them to review it, then set a time to go over it with them. Zoom works very well here as you can share the estimate on the screen and go through it with them, and they can see what you're talking about as they listen.

No one knew their home better than they did. Go over the estimate draft with them and correct any items that may not match details of their home. For example, are there too many windows in a room? Note the page number, line item in question, and a small description of the item that needs to be corrected, deleted, or added. Don't have them worry about cubic yards of cement, roofing trusses, etc. Have them focus on the items one can see: windows, floors, trim, etc.

Take these corrections and update the report. After it is as accurate as possible, put the base report together with any substantiating documents like photos, plans, interviews, invoices, etc.

8. What is my alternative to using Xactimate to prove my loss?

An insurance company needs details, but to date, not a single company we know of specifies in their policies that those details must come in the form of Xactimate. In our opinion, as a contractor, if you can provide an estimate with supporting documentation (invoices, past work receipts, price lists from supply stores, etc.), the insurance company has no right to demand the data be represented only in Xactimate.

9. What next?

Once you have an accurate, detailed estimate ready, the claimant needs to share it with their insurance company and get an agreement on the MOI. Read Chapter 2 for more on this topic.

Once the MOI has been agreed on, it is much easier for the claimant to sign a fix-bid building contract with a builder. If they can't get clarity on MOI, it is difficult to determine how they will pay a builder. Because if they can't be sure how much the insurance company will cover, how can they ask for a construction loan or determine if they have enough in savings? Also, for those who have policies which may also allow the purchase of a replacement home, the MOI provides a clear budget number for the purchase of an already-built home.

The above paragraph explains why we keep coming back to MOI. This number clarifies the loss and at the same time, removes all the ambiguity of the claim. Now the claimant knows their loss and what their coverage should be.

Usually, within a month or two from the fire or damages, claimants are provided with a large sum of money that is called the "indisputable amount" (or "Actual Cash Value"). They may have more coverage available, but they are given this amount to start a clock ticking on the claim and to help them hire a builder and get rebuilding.

To obtain further coverage amounts, they will have to prove they have spent the indisputable amount dollars on building. A good builder will track costs, provide proof that the building costs have exceeded the initial payout, and help the claimant obtain the remaining coverages available.

You can be a hero or a hindrance in this part of the claim. If you can track expenses, keep invoices, and prove that costs have been incurred and that they were incurred on the rebuilding of the home that was damaged, the company is usually obliged to pay out in stages (typically when you've completed foundation, framing, closed in, completion of home) until they have paid out the maximum amount covered in the policy.

Along the way, the company may question expenses. This is where you can show them the estimate created before building started, and then show them the invoices for the work that has been completed and some photos to prove it.

This is sometimes frustrating, always takes longer than it should, and is not a normal part of how you have ever built a home.

But by this point you've learned; we don't ask why. We ask how. Your town has been devastated by a disaster. Your neighbors need the help to prove the value of their losses.

How can you help? Only a quality builder can provide this data. If you provide accurate data, in a format acceptable to an insurance company, you are going to accelerate the recovery of your community. People will get insurance proceeds faster, you can build more homes, and your community's economic recovery can begin in earnest.

*Opinions in this book must never be considered legal, tax, insurance, or claims advice in any way. Always check our opinions with your professional advisor. We share our knowledge only in the spirit of sharing of information educationally.

About the Authors

Bill grew up in Sonoma County and has been on build sites since he was a teenager. Today he's a successful entrepreneur, owning and operating BW Builder and West Coast Diesels, a truck repair company.

Matt spent 25 years in the financial services industry and during that time, became proficient at understanding the most efficient ways to get insurance companies to work with their clients. He is also the co-founder of the startup company www.illuminote.io, a company that helps individuals protect and control their most important financial documents. He has enjoyed helping disaster survivors and hopes more contractors will take this model to help their towns.

www.ingramcontent.com/pod-product-compliance
Lightning Source LLC
Chambersburg PA
CBHW070031030426

42335CB00017B/2387